# MODERNISM IN CONTEXT

HOMES BY LIONEL MORRISON

*To Phyliss and Edward Meyerson, who inspired and encouraged me to pursue architecture as a career, and to Nancy Chatmas, whose love and support allowed it to happen.*

*And finally, to Susan Seifert, my forever partner in work and life, whose inspiration and collaboration brought out the best in me.*

*Thank you all for your inestimable contributions to the work shown herein as well as the rest of my work that is not a part of this book.*

Lionel Morrison

Foreword by Nate Eudaly Introduction by Lucilo Peña

# MODERNISM IN CONTEXT

## HOMES BY LIONEL MORRISON

images
Publishing

# Contents

## Foreword

By Nate Eudaly, Hon. AIA
Executive Director, Dallas Architecture Forum

On the axes where inspired modern architecture and timeless design meet, Mies van der Rohe and Le Corbusier stand as twin pillars. Other architects have also produced bodies of work that merit inclusion at this important juncture, but that distinction is rare. Lionel Morrison, FAIA, has certainly earned that recognition, as the projects in this book conclusively attest.

Each of Morrison's residences is unique, yet they exemplify underlying design principles that signal a "Lionel Morrison residence." Exteriors and interiors will almost always be in his signature white, with orthogonality creating a refined grid for the structure. Carefully sited with a limited material palette of steel, glass, and stone combined with highly polished concrete and rift-cut white oak, Morrison's designs produce elegant, exacting, and serene environments for contemporary living.

Light is used judiciously in Morrison's homes to avoid the harsh southwestern sun while bringing diffused illumination into interior spaces. Strategically placed light wells, courtyards, clerestory windows, window walls, and translucent glass all achieve ethereal illumination.

Water is also an integral part of the residences in this collection. Thoughtfully using this scarce resource, Morrison creates water features as focal points. Whether they are small fountains, flowing water, reflecting pools, or lap pools, they all provide expressions of refreshment and subtle movement that enhance a sense of serenity.

A modified cruciform design is used in many of the buildings, where an interior courtyard or body of water is positioned at the center of the house with rooms radiating out on each side. Throughout Morrison's houses, doors and windows are carefully placed to frame views of the next points of discovery. The Berkshire Residence is a prime example of this. As one approaches the entrance in the evening, both exterior and interior lighting bathe the view with an atmosphere of mystery, inviting the visitor to explore its dramatic spaces. A full-height window purposefully sited in the master bedroom provides a vista across the courtyard to glimpse the sculpture in the opposite wing. Views in all of Morrison's homes are intentionally situated to provide new points of discovery throughout both the interiors and exteriors.

Morrison gives functional rooms pride of place, creating serendipitous design encounters. I vividly remember the first time I entered the compact powder room of the Glendora Residence. Turning to face the sink, it felt like I had entered a small private chapel. Under a narrow skylight and spotlight, a custom-crafted, square, concrete vanity anchored the end of the room. An orchid appeared to be suspended in air midway between the spotlight and the round basin, completing this subdued and contemplative atmosphere. Washing my hands in this chamber was not mundane but restorative for my senses. Similar effects are achieved with the kitchen sink as a dramatic focal point in the Avondale Residence, and the sculptural bathtub with the backdrop of floor-to-ceiling stone at the Bassi Ranch Residence. In addition, small wall alcoves throughout Morrison's houses create enhanced views for both sculpture and paintings.

As with Le Corbusier's residences, Lionel Morrison's body of work is distinguished and elegantly austere. Over my two decades as Executive Director of the Dallas Architecture Forum, I have gained the greater understanding that Morrison is, like his work, thoughtful, intentional, and gracious. He not only strives for excellence, he achieves enduring quality.

I invite you to enjoy these amazing homes that exemplify modernism with timeless context.

## Introduction

By Lucilo Peña
President of Development, Billingsley Company

Shortly after I moved back to Dallas in November 1996, a friend invited me to his home for a holiday party—it was in Lionel Morrison's Princeton Residence, one of the stunning homes featured in this monograph. As an architect and real estate developer, I was impressed by the thoughtful design, the quality of the details, the dialogue between the architecture and the exterior, and the elegant proportions of the spaces. Days later, I contacted Morrison, and that was the beginning of a long and productive relationship, which resulted in many award-winning office and mixed-use projects.

The residences in this monograph feature an architecture derived from its context, primarily site and program. For example, a clear contextual response to the urban fabric can be seen at One Arts Plaza, where Morrison uses the square as a leitmotif, layering it to anchor the east end of Flora Street, the main axis of the Dallas Arts District, at the first and top levels. The facade setbacks of the buildings along Flora Street are extended into the site and expressed by open fin walls that create a large public plaza on the first level, surrounded by restaurants with outdoor seating. The form of the building is a rational response to the site; it couldn't coherently exist anywhere else.

Context also refers to the topography, natural features, and overall environment. Most of Morrison's work is in Texas and responds to its traditions, landscape, and climate. Shading devices provide shelter from the natural light and heat—canopies are employed, roofs are extended, and trellises are used to filter the sun. Standing-seam metal roofs are used, which evolved from durable roofs common in Texas ranch buildings. Interiors connect with the outside through large windows where the visual connection is further strengthened by interior floor patterns that continue to the outside. For example, in some cases granite slabs become pavers, and interior walls extend outdoors to embrace courtyards and become stacked limestone features.

Morrison creates clear, elegant solutions in a very modern vocabulary where form follows function, and applied ornamentation is avoided: his is an architecture of essentials. The designs are classical in the true essence of the word and emphasize harmony, balance, and proportion. Meticulous thought is given to axial arrangements, spatial flow, balanced compositions, and light as a design element. The employment of available materials includes marble, granite, limestone, wood, and other durable materials commonly used in classical architecture. Vistas are framed, and the relationship between architecture and landscape is explored where interiors and exteriors frequently blend and influence each other, be they courtyards, gardens, or pools.

Morrison's sense of classical design is also applied to his lobbies, which are treated like gallery spaces designed to display art. They are places of beauty and durability finished in timeless materials; spaces that are also in dialogue with their exteriors.

The term "classical architecture" applies to any mode of architecture that has evolved to a highly refined state. In that sense, Lionel Morrison's work is classically modern, both timeless and contemporary.

## Beechwood Residence

Dallas, Texas
1994

The Beechwood Residence was designed for a single client, whose previous townhouse in Dallas's Oak Lawn area we had also created. For this new home, the client requested a typical program with one notable exception: a well-appointed home office, as he primarily worked remotely. Additionally, the design needed to be able to accommodate the potential needs of a future spouse—a prescient consideration, as he married during the later stages of construction.

The site, a flat, 1-acre property, is expansive for a house of just 3,200 square feet. To ensure the design harmonized with its surroundings, we chose to keep the house to a single level, but with double-height, slanted ceilings in the living area, and align it parallel to the long street frontage. This approach allowed the residence to sit comfortably on the site while establishing a strong physical presence.

From the street, the composition presents three distinct planes: a gray steel roof, a white stucco wall, and a vibrant green lawn, all set against the expanse of the blue Texas sky. The house, enclosed within a single-gable form, is closed to the street for privacy, but opens generously to the private outdoor space at the rear of the property. Architectural inflections at the entryway and the master suite subtly announce their functions, while a vertically prominent limestone-clad chimney emphasizes the entry and serves as the terminus of the processional pathway leading to the home.

The arrival experience is carefully choreographed. Guests park in an area that invites a gradual discovery of the house, transitioning from the public domain of the street to the private sanctuary within.

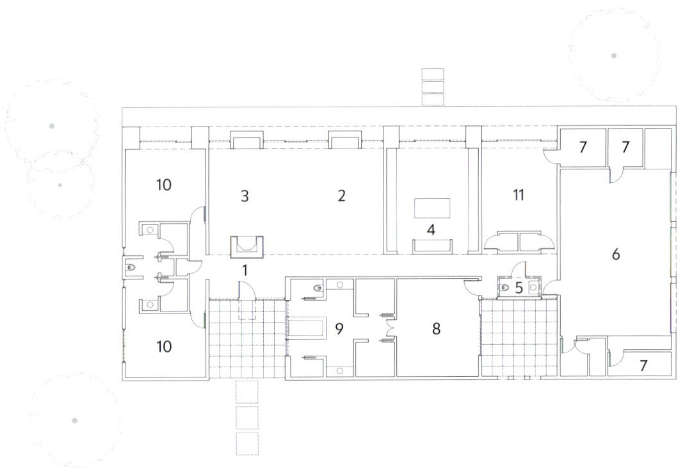


1 Entry
2 Dining room
3 Living room
4 Kitchen
5 Powder room
6 Garage
7 Storage
8 Master bedroom
9 Master bathroom
10 Bedroom
11 Study

0 20 ft

Floor plan

Several innovative design details were introduced for the first time in this residence. These include a standing-seam steel roof constructed of continuous panels without intermediate joints, a roofline that integrates seamlessly into a concealed gutter system flush with the facade, and an internal drainage system discharging discreetly at the base of the front wall. Additionally, polished concrete floors are visually separated from the walls by a continuous reveal, and trimless doors are set into surrounding quarter-inch reveals for a clean, modern aesthetic.

Natural light plays a pivotal role in the design. A south-facing, deeply recessed glass wall opens to the rear outdoor space, while high gable windows on the north side introduce diffused light into the main living areas. Translucent glass in the master bathroom and powder room balances illumination and privacy, while a private terrace off the master suite provides soft natural light and views of the surrounding neighborhood.

The Beechwood Residence is an exploration of mystery and surprise. Its unassuming, blind facade conceals the luminous, light-filled spaces within—delivering a delightful contrast for those who step inside.

# Princeton Residence

Highland Park, Texas
1994

The Princeton Residence and the Beechwood Residence were conceived simultaneously, sharing an almost identical program. Despite this, the two homes differ significantly in form, a reflection of the distinct opportunities and constraints of their respective sites, as well as the aesthetic preferences of their owners.

The client for the Princeton Residence sought to blend his appreciation for Texas Hill Country architecture, and its emphasis on local materials and functionality, with his desire for a modern home. The challenge lay in honoring traditional architectural elements while interpreting them through a contemporary lens.

Located on a 50-foot-wide infill lot in the charming enclave of Highland Park, the house spans two stories and is positioned along the eastern edge of the property. This arrangement preserves the western portion for a courtyard and swimming pool, creating a harmonious balance between built and open spaces.

Access to the home is thoughtfully arranged: the owner enters from the alley at the rear, while guests are welcomed from the street. Facing the street, the house presents a monumental porch, a modern abstraction of Hill Country porches. The porch's back wall is clad in Texas limestone, referencing the traditional material but rendered with a smooth finish and a stacked bond pattern. A subtle line of uplights begins on the porch and continues into the home's interior, illuminating the stone wall and enhancing its presence.

The entry sequence is intentionally planned. Visitors first step into a gallery, passing through the stone wall to access the main living spaces, the stairway to the upper floor, and the courtyard beyond. The second floor, housing the bedrooms, features a recessed balcony overlooking the courtyard and pool.

The living and dining areas open seamlessly to the courtyard through a full-height glass wall with sliding panels, creating an uninterrupted flow between interior and exterior spaces. Columnar magnolias, their white springtime blooms complementing the home's color palette, line the western edge of the courtyard.

The kitchen, situated at the rear near the garage, includes a private garden that brings in natural light and offers a quiet retreat. Ascending the stairway reveals a composed view over the pool and garden. The visual axis culminates in the single construction of the outdoor fireplace and chimney, which is paired with a white stucco wall that serves as a backdrop for a carefully selected specimen of Japanese maple.

The Princeton Residence is a bold yet harmonious modern reinterpretation of a historic architectural style. Its crisp, rigorous design fits seamlessly into its surroundings, offering a thoughtful balance of tradition and contemporary living.

## Glendora Residence

Dallas, Texas
1995

The Glendora Residence was commissioned by a family of three—a couple and their teenage son—who approached us with a passion for modernism and a deep appreciation for Spanish architecture and culture. Their lifestyle emphasized frequent entertaining, which shaped the program alongside their additional requests for a pool, cabana, and maid's quarters.

Drawing inspiration from the clients' love of Spanish architecture and their need for a space well suited to entertaining, we developed a courtyard scheme. The house itself defines the courtyard, creating a seamless relationship between the interior and exterior spaces. This design is perfectly suited for both daily living and hosting gatherings of varying sizes.

The site of the house is a half-acre lot on a tree-lined street in Preston Hollow, one of Dallas's most desirable neighborhoods. The house is positioned deep into the site, away from the street, to preserve the existing tree canopy and harmonize with the neighborhood. A blind street frontage and tall wall add an air of mystery while safeguarding the privacy of the courtyard and interior spaces.

The entrance gate is subtly concealed from the street view, with a cantilevered cover hinting at its presence and providing shelter for visitors. Upon entry, the journey to the front door takes one past the pool, with the view terminated by a striking sculpture.

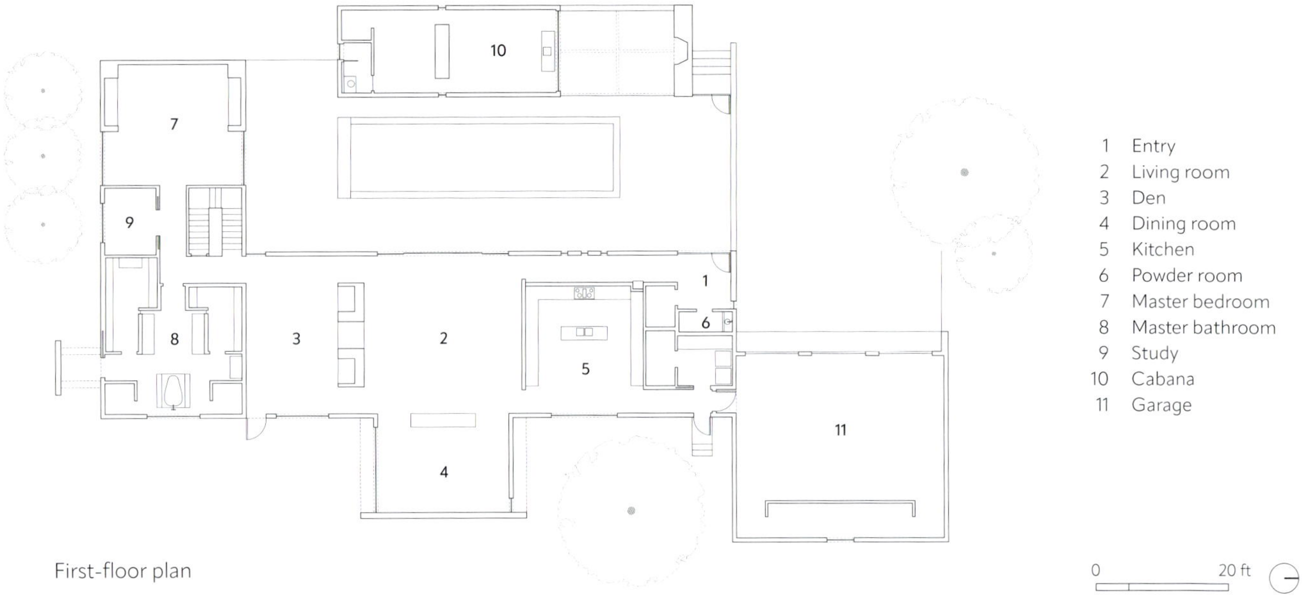


1 Entry
2 Living room
3 Den
4 Dining room
5 Kitchen
6 Powder room
7 Master bedroom
8 Master bathroom
9 Study
10 Cabana
11 Garage

First-floor plan

Inside, a narrow gallery leads to the main living and dining space, where the transition from polished concrete floors to limestone and an increase in ceiling height signal a shift in spatial rhythm. A freestanding fireplace delineates the living area from the den, which lies adjacent to the master suite and the stairway leading to the upstairs bedrooms. The master suite is thoughtfully designed along a long axis that culminates in a tranquil view of an outdoor sculpture. A sliding glass panel in the master bedroom offers unencumbered access to the courtyard and pool.

The material palette enhances the home's refined yet grounded aesthetic. Exterior stucco walls, polished concrete and limestone floors on the first level, white oak floors upstairs, rosewood cabinetry, and honed green slate in the master bathroom create a cohesive and luxurious environment.

The Glendora Residence is defined by its interplay of form, space, light, and landscape. Its design not only reflects the owners' tastes but also provides a versatile and engaging space for both living and entertaining.

1 Bedroom
2 Bathroom
3 Study
4 Roof

Second-floor plan

0 20 ft

4331
4333
4335
4337

## Travis Street Townhouses

Dallas, Texas
2001

The Travis Street Townhouses project marks the fourth collaboration with a client renowned for the Vanguard Way residential development, also featured in this collection. For this project, the developer selected an infill lot in Dallas's dynamic Oak Lawn neighborhood, an area transitioning from neglected housing stock to a hub of luxury residences and high-end retail.

The project comprises four 3,400-square-foot townhouses organized around a serene, shared courtyard. This courtyard, enhanced by a rusted-steel water feature, serves as a tranquil gateway, inviting visitors from the bustling urban surroundings into the privacy of the homes.

A defining aspect of the design is the sequence of transitions. Residents and visitors enter through a secure gate into the central courtyard, where the gentle sound of flowing water establishes a sense of calm. From there, private garden entries lead to the homes' interiors, culminating in the primary living spaces on the second floor, which overlook private gardens and the shared courtyard. This spatial layering reinforces an indoor–outdoor connection throughout the property.

Each townhouse features three levels. The first floor houses the entry and master suite, the second floor contains the primary living spaces, and the third floor accommodates two additional bedrooms. Roof terraces provide sweeping views of the neighborhood and the Downtown Dallas skyline. Open riser stairways flood the interiors with natural light and frame views of the surrounding green spaces.

The design emphasizes harmony with its urban context. The townhouses incorporate two- and three-story elements, with the lower two-story sections positioned along the street to blend seamlessly into the streetscape. The dark-colored stucco further enhances this integration.

Innovative use of materials adds to the project's character. While the concrete structures remain hidden beneath exterior stucco and interior drywall, they ensure durability and energy efficiency. Polished concrete floors throughout, ebonized wenge woodwork, and statuary white marble in the bathrooms contribute to the refined material palette.

Particularly notable is the emphasis on the indoor–outdoor connection, exemplified in the master bathroom. Operable glass walls on either side open onto private green spaces, offering the unique experience of bathing in nature while enjoying the comfort of an enclosed, climate-controlled environment.

The Travis Street Townhouses offer a sanctuary of calm and privacy within the lively energy of the Oak Lawn neighborhood—an exceptional balance of urban living and serene retreat.

# Berkshire Residence

Dallas, Texas
2004

Inspired by their visit to the Glendora Residence, the clients set out to create a modern home of their own. Their search led to a half-acre site in a traditional North Dallas neighborhood, offering both significant advantages and distinct challenges.

The site's most notable feature was the stand of mature oak trees gracing the front of the property. However, a busy thoroughfare at the rear presented a considerable obstacle. In response, the design evolved into a U-shaped plan, turning its back on the thoroughfare and embracing a courtyard as its heart. Shaded by the existing tree canopy and oriented to the southern sky, the courtyard serves as a serene and private focal point, with the house itself shielding it from noise and disruption.

This 5,000-square-foot home situates all primary living spaces on the first floor, while guest bedrooms and a balcony overlook the courtyard from the second floor. The journey from the street to front door is one of discovery, beginning with a broken pathway that leads beside a tall, sentinel-like wall to a mahogany gate framed by translucent glass sidelights. Beyond the gate, a covered pathway flanking the courtyard guides visitors to the front entrance. Once inside, a gallery opens onto an outdoor sculpture garden, setting the stage for the home's thoughtful and layered spatial experience. The main living space offers an axial perspective of the courtyard and pool, unifying the design concept.

Large sliding doors in the living area, along with walls that recede in the master suite and cabana, blur the line between indoor and outdoor environments. This seamless integration makes the home ideal for the daily lives of its two residents and for hosting large-scale events. The courtyard also provides a flexible venue for displaying and rotating the owners' outdoor furniture and fabric collections.

Key materials enhance the home's character and cohesiveness. Floors and courtyards feature polished concrete with a grid of inset limestone, while cabinetry is crafted from ebonized wenge wood. The exterior is rendered in a subtle gray-green stucco, with walls and ceilings finished in our signature white. The dark exterior tone enables the home to blend harmoniously with the surrounding oak trees, visually softening its scale.

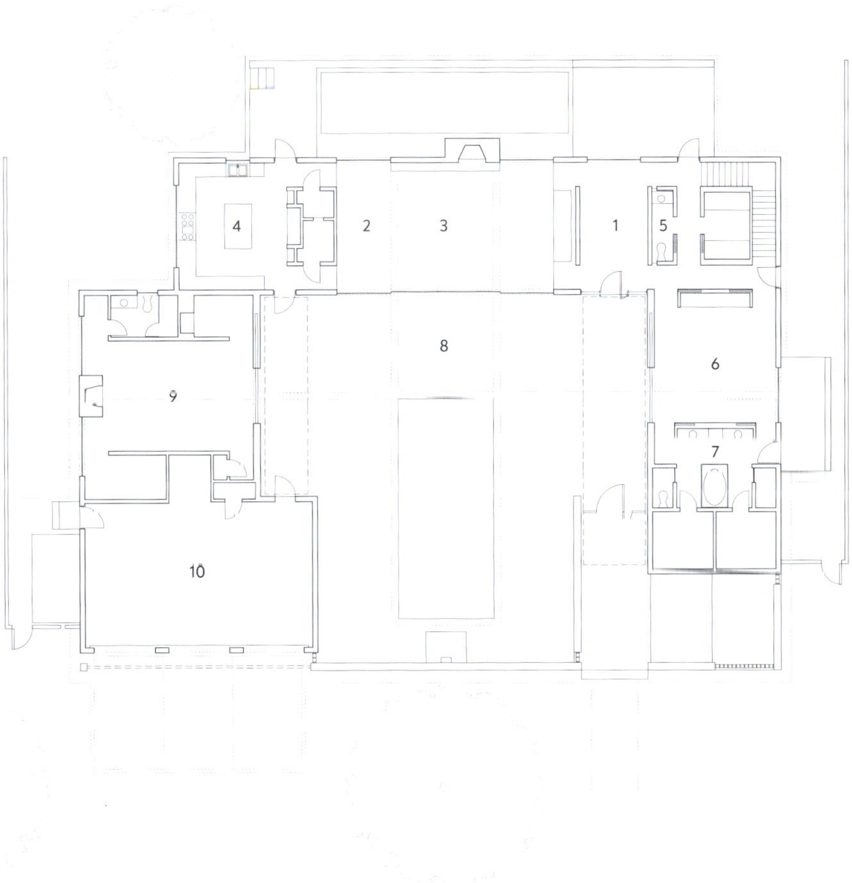


1 Entry
2 Dining room
3 Living room
4 Kitchen
5 Powder room
6 Master bedroom
7 Master bathroom
8 Courtyard
9 Studio/Guest room
10 Garage

First-floor plan

0 20 ft

1 Bedroom
2 Bathroom
3 Storage
4 Balcony
5 Roof

Second-floor plan

0 20 ft

As the neighborhood's only modern home, and largest house, the Berkshire Residence is a respectful and elegant addition. Its thoughtful design ensures it nestles naturally under the canopy of oaks and the vast Texas sky.

## Versailles Residence

Highland Park, Texas
2004

The Versailles Residence was born from the owners' desire to move from Far North Dallas to Highland Park, widely celebrated as one of the most beautiful areas in Dallas. Their search led them to North Versailles Avenue , a picturesque boulevard featuring a charming urban park within its median. Naturally, the owners wanted their home to embrace and engage with this exceptional setting.

In response, we oriented the design to establish a direct connection with the park. Principal living spaces were elevated to the second floor, offering unobstructed views of the park while fostering a meaningful relationship with the surrounding neighborhood. The master suite and office also occupy the second floor, each with access to private outdoor spaces. Meanwhile, the entry, guest suites, and an intimate garden are situated on the first floorl.

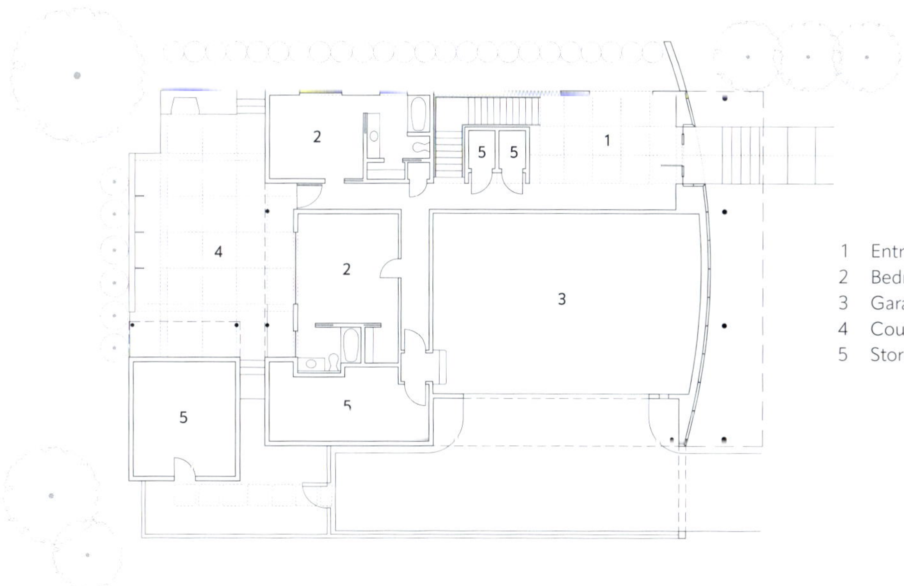


1 Entry
2 Bedroom
3 Garage
4 Courtyard
5 Storage

First-floor plan

0 20 ft

A single, expansive volume houses the living, dining, and den spaces, with a view to the park through a sweeping, floor-to-ceiling curved wall of metal and glass. This feature invites panoramic views of the lush landscape and neighborhood beyond. The home's centerline organizes the dining room, kitchen, and terrace along a linear axis, ensuring these spaces enjoy views of both the park and the private rear garden.

The roof, supported by freestanding steel columns and surrounded by glass on all sides, appears to float above the main living space. This striking design detail reads as an independent, protective element that shelters the structure below.

Visitors entering the home encounter a dramatic two-story wall of translucent glass, allowing the interior to be bathed in soft, diffused light while maintaining complete privacy. Ascending the stairway along this luminous wall, guests arrive at the second-floor spaces, which unfold to reveal stunning, framed views of the park.

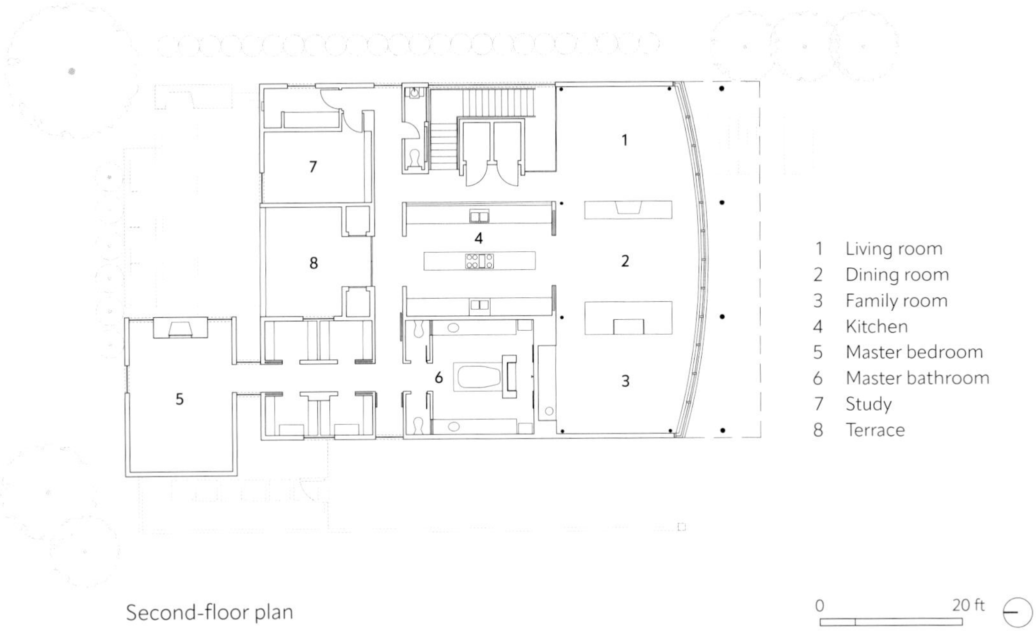


Second-floor plan

The 5,000-square-foot residence is crafted from a sophisticated material palette. Texas limestone, painted structural steel, white stucco, and a gray, standing-seam metal roof define the exterior. Inside, white oak floors, maple cabinetry, French limestone baths, and walls and ceilings rendered in our signature white complete the refined aesthetic.

Though we often design from the inside out, the Versailles Residence was conceived from the outside in, allowing the home to fully embrace its unique context. The result is a harmonious balance of form, light, and landscape that celebrates its relationship with the park and its surroundings.

## Arthouse Residences

Dallas, Texas
2005

The idea for the Arthouse Residences originated from a conversation with our client for the Glendora Residence, also included in this book. He proposed adapting the architectural language of his private residence for the multifamily market, a concept I wholeheartedly supported. Thus began our search for the perfect site.

We selected a corner lot at Holland Avenue and Oak Lawn Avenue, ideally situated in the vibrant Oak Lawn neighborhood and just a block from Turtle Creek, one of Dallas's most historic and picturesque areas.

The Arthouse Residences were designed as a cohesive architectural entity, not a fragmented composition of individual units. The structure features eight condominium apartments, each approximately 2,300 square feet, arranged across two levels. The first floor includes a lobby and parking for residents and their guests.

Residents access their apartments via an elevator leading to the second or third floor, where the apartments surround a dramatic, double-height central space. This skylit atrium, with a bridge on the third floor for additional access, offers an extraordinary communal experience hidden from the building's exterior.

The Arthouse Residences offer two apartment layouts. Second-floor units feature two bedrooms and a den, with private terraces along the perimeter. Third-floor units enjoy the added benefit of central atria, allowing light and air to penetrate their interiors. Open floor plans emphasize connections across living spaces and between the living areas and master suites. Discreet, recessed rolling shades provide privacy when desired.

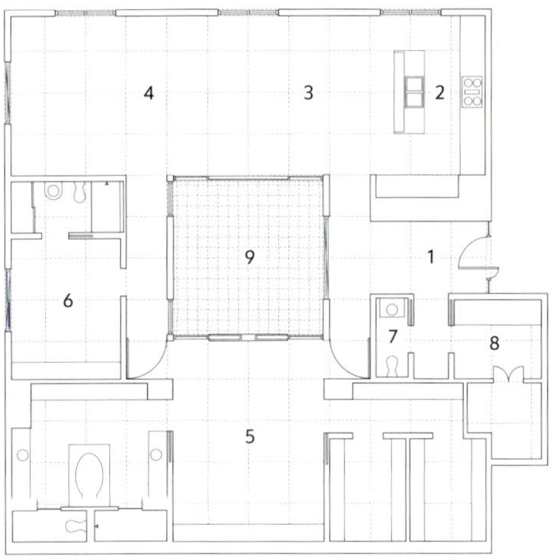


1 Entry
2 Dining room
3 Living room
4 Kitchen
5 Master suite
6 Guest suite
7 Powder room
8 Laundry
9 Atrium

Third-floor apartment plan

0 20 ft

The main living spaces are open and adaptable, enabling residents to tailor their loft-like apartments to individual tastes. United by their passion for art and architecture, residents have personalized their homes in unique yet harmonious ways.

The building's exterior combines burnished concrete block and exposed concrete with white stucco. Interior finishes include concrete flooring, rift-cut white oak cabinetry, stainless-steel countertops, and statuary white and Thassos marble in the bathrooms. The walls and ceilings are rendered in our signature white, further uniting the design.

51

# Vanguard Way Residence

Dallas, Texas
2006

The Vanguard Way Residence was commissioned by the first buyers in a groundbreaking Dallas residential development dedicated exclusively to modern architecture. Situated on a site overlooking a beautiful public parkway and adjacent to the Dallas Area Rapid Transit (DART) line, the home embraces its dynamic urban context.

In addition to traditional program components, the owners required an office, media room, and photographic studio. The design resolved these needs across two levels: the primary living spaces occupy the first floor, while the guest suite, office, and media room are located on the second floor. The garage was specifically designed to double as a functional photographic studio, adding flexibility to the program.

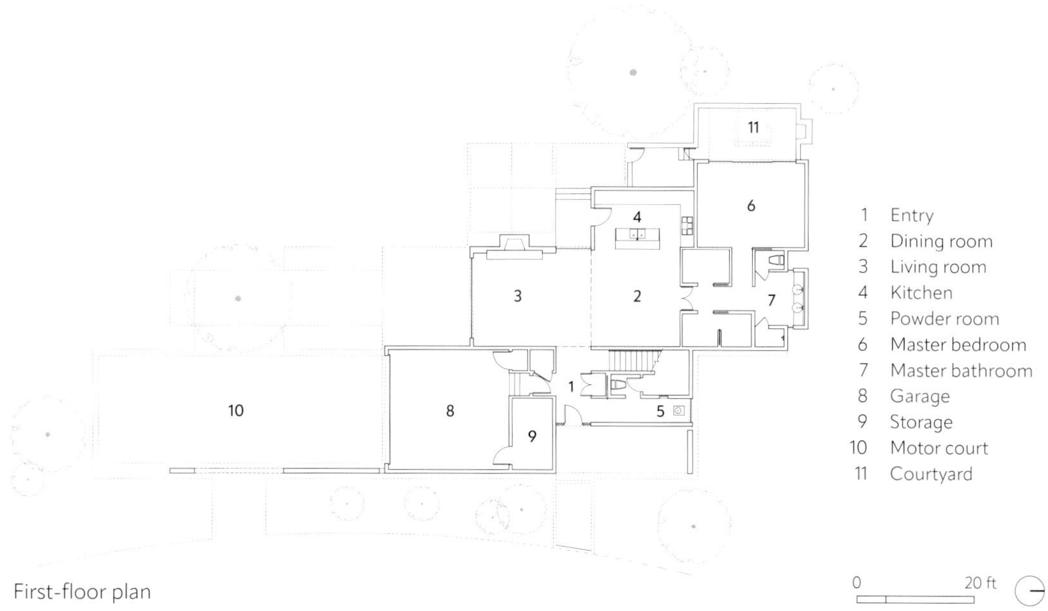


First-floor plan

The house, rendered in smooth white stucco, perches on a cliff above the parkway. It celebrates its proximity to the DART, with the passing trains adding vibrancy to the surrounding environment. In accordance with design covenants, the residence is positioned close to the street. Guests may park on the street or within the motor court before entering a dramatic double-height space that includes the powder room—an element thoughtfully integrated into the entry sequence.

Moving past the stairway, the space compresses briefly before opening into the expansive double-height living room. Adjacent to this space, the dining room is defined by a more intimate ceiling height, offering a distinct yet connected experience. Beyond the dining room lies the master bathroom and bedroom, which open onto a private courtyard. Though outdoor space is limited on the site, dedicated areas such as the master-suite courtyard and a sculpture platform between the living room and parkway enhance the design's connection to the outdoors.

Second-floor plan

The elevated position of the house allows the owners to enjoy privacy while observing the active parkway below, frequented by walkers, joggers, and cyclists. This interplay between public and private realms exemplifies the thoughtful planning of the home.

The material palette reinforces the modern aesthetic and functionality of the house. Key finishes include polished concrete floors, statuary white marble in the bathrooms, maple cabinetry, and smooth walls and ceilings.

The Vanguard Way Residence exemplifies modern living within an urban setting, achieving a balance of ease, privacy, and connection to the lively public realm.

# One Arts Plaza Penthouse

Dallas, Texas
2006

The journey of One Arts Plaza began with an exciting call from a client, marking the award of a project that would occupy a pivotal site at the edge of the Dallas Arts District. This district is home to world-renowned performing and fine arts venues, many designed by Pritzker Prize–winning architects. At its heart lies Flora Street, the axis that organizes the district, stretching from the Dallas Museum of Art in the west to One Arts Plaza at the eastern end.

One Arts Plaza is a mixed-use development, seamlessly combining retail spaces on the first level, office spaces above, and residential condominiums crowning the structure. The residential component begins with its own dedicated first-floor lobby, distinct from other functions within the development. This lobby not only serves as a welcoming space but is itself an art venue, designed with dark-stained oak flooring, satin stainless-steel elevator doors, translucent glass, and Thassos marble cladding the elevator core walls. A reception desk of statuary white marble and stainless steel provides a striking focal point.

Residents of One Arts Plaza enjoy sweeping views of the Dallas skyline and the Arts District, along with shared amenities such as a swimming pool overlooking Downtown Dallas, Uptown, and the district itself.

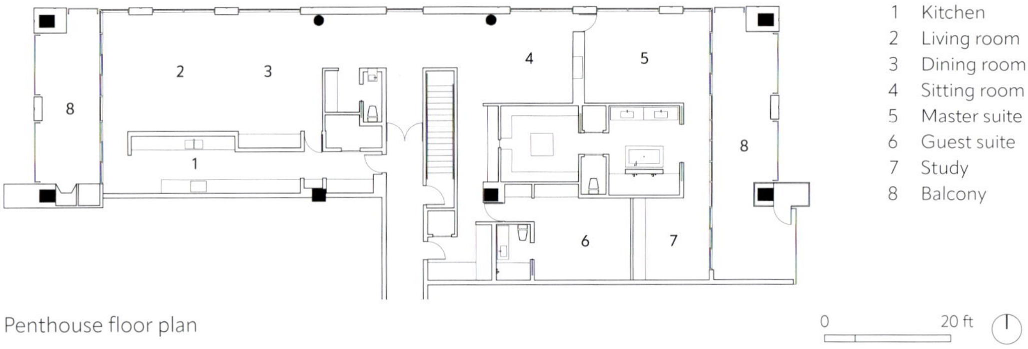


Penthouse floor plan

One of the owners of the penthouse featured here played a pivotal role in commissioning the project. The design of their residence captures breathtaking views while serving as a showcase for their classic modern furnishings and their impressive and evolving art collection.

Primary living spaces are spacious and fitted with full-height perimeter glass, maximizing the spectacular vistas. The Bulthaup kitchen, with its sleek honed granite countertops and aluminum cabinetry, opens directly onto a terrace featuring an outdoor fireplace and panoramic views of the Arts District.

The master bathroom exemplifies the advantages of its top-floor location, featuring a skylight that floods a full-height wall of white marble with natural light, illuminating both the bathroom and adjoining wardrobes. In the sitting room, a fireplace is framed by a white marble wall accented with translucent glass, defining the entrance to the master suite.

Interior finishes reflect a thoughtful blend of luxury and minimalism, incorporating charcoal stone flooring, rift-cut white oak cabinetry, statuary white marble, and walls and ceilings finished in our signature white.

Both the broader development and this penthouse encapsulate a harmonious balance between public and private art. One Arts Plaza serves as a conduit for residents to connect with world-class architecture, culture, and the abundant amenities of Dallas.

4430

## Abbott Residence

Dallas, Texas
2007

Situated on a 7,500-square-foot corner lot in the Northern Hills neighborhood of Dallas, the Abbott Residence enjoys high visibility and proximity to Highland Park. The nearby Katy Trail, one of Dallas's premier amenities, is accessible at the end of Abbott Avenue.

While the location is highly desirable, zoning requirements for dual front-yard setbacks posed a challenge, significantly reducing the buildable area. To overcome this, the 4,400-square-foot residence was designed on two levels, strategically positioned along the northern edge of the property. This layout reserves the southern portion for a serene outdoor space featuring a pool, spa, and courtyard, which form the heart of the home's outdoor living area.

The facade combines contemporary design with functionality. Floor-to-ceiling glazing spans both levels, shielded by a teak lattice that adds shading, privacy, and texture to the front elevation. The structure's mass cantilevers toward the street, a design echoed by the steps leading to the entry platform. A wall separating the spa from the entryway extends into the house, guiding visitors into the interior.

The first floor accommodates the main living areas, including the entry, dining room, living room, media room, and kitchen. These spaces seamlessly connect to the courtyard through a full-height glass wall with sliding panels, allowing direct access to the outdoor entertainment areas. The southern edge of the courtyard is lined with 'Claudia Wannamaker' magnolias, an evergreen variety that ensures year-round privacy, texture, and seasonal bursts of white flowers.

The upper level offers a library overlooking the street, followed by two versatile rooms that can serve as bedrooms, home offices, or other functional spaces. These rooms open to a balcony with views of the pool and courtyard below. The eastern end houses the master suite, which features a thoughtfully designed bathroom with a central lavatory area. A light-filled shower, illuminated by large, translucent windows, connects the two vanities.

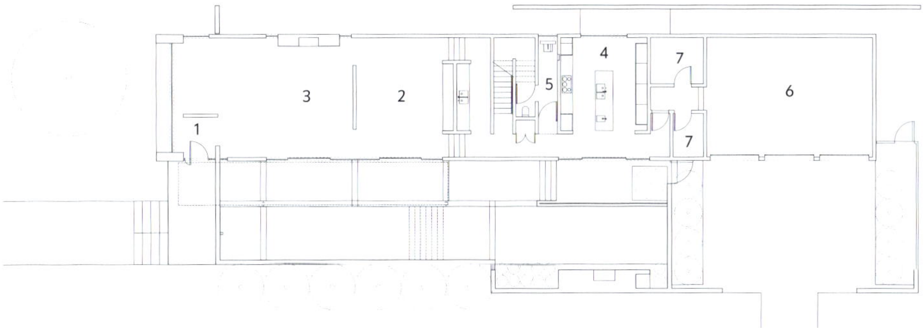

1 Entry
2 Dining room
3 Living room
4 Kitchen
5 Powder room
6 Garage
7 Storage

First-floor plan

0 20 ft

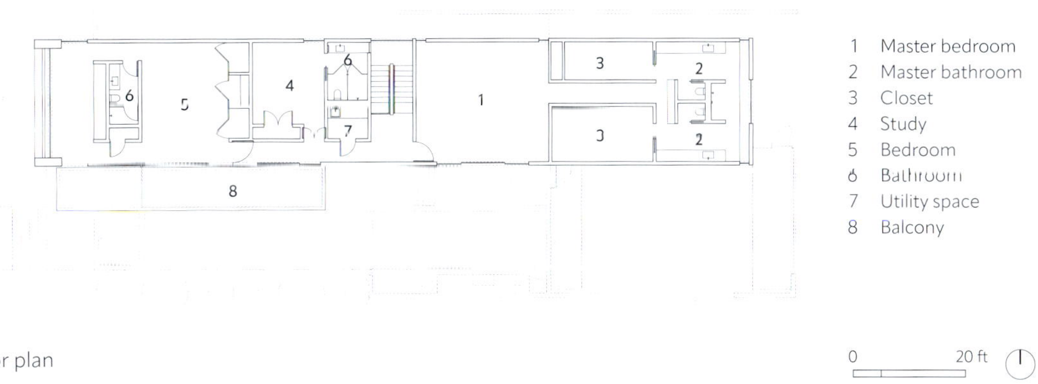


1 Master bedroom
2 Master bathroom
3 Closet
4 Study
5 Bedroom
6 Bathroom
7 Utility space
8 Balcony

Second-floor plan

The Abbott Residence's material palette blends sophistication and durability. Exterior finishes include smooth white stucco, teak for screening, stainless-steel accents, and concrete and limestone paving. Inside, the house features concrete flooring, stainless-steel countertops, ebonized wenge cabinetry, translucent glass, and bathrooms clad in statuary white and Thassos marble.

This residence exemplifies creative design solutions for optimizing a constrained site, delivering a light-filled, modern home with a strong connection to its outdoor environment.

4430

## Avondale Residence

Dallas, Texas
2015

The Avondale Residence is a thoughtfully designed family home nestled in the prestigious Turtle Creek area of Dallas, Texas. Positioned on an 8,075-square-foot parcel of irregular shape with significant topographical challenges, the site's modest size, unique contours, and the preservation of a grand old oak tree guided the creative process.

Designed to blend functionality with elegance, the residence fulfills the clients' desire for a home suited for work, entertaining, and hosting overnight guests. The layout seamlessly merges the interior with the private outdoor courtyard and pool, maximizing both space and usability.

4347

The home's street-facing elevation embodies a sense of privacy with a primarily honed Roman travertine facade. Chosen for its timeless texture and tone, the stone harmonizes with the white stucco exterior, and its rainscreen installation ensures durability and aesthetic longevity. This wall, which minimizes street noise, is punctuated only by a glass vitrine that provides a curated view of the neighborhood from the kitchen.

The kitchen, realized in collaboration with German manufacturer Bulthaup, reflects a commitment to refined modernity. Strategically positioned skylights in the kitchen and master bathroom flood the interiors with natural light, enhancing features like the full-height statuary white marble wall. Borrowed light through translucent glass illuminates the powder and dining rooms, adding subtle elegance.

Inside, expansive sliding glass panels blur the boundaries between the interior living spaces and the courtyard, creating a harmonious indoor–outdoor connection. The interior finishes include diamond-polished concrete floors, statuary white marble countertops, and rift-cut white oak cabinetry. Walls and ceilings, painted in our signature white, complement the serene aesthetic.

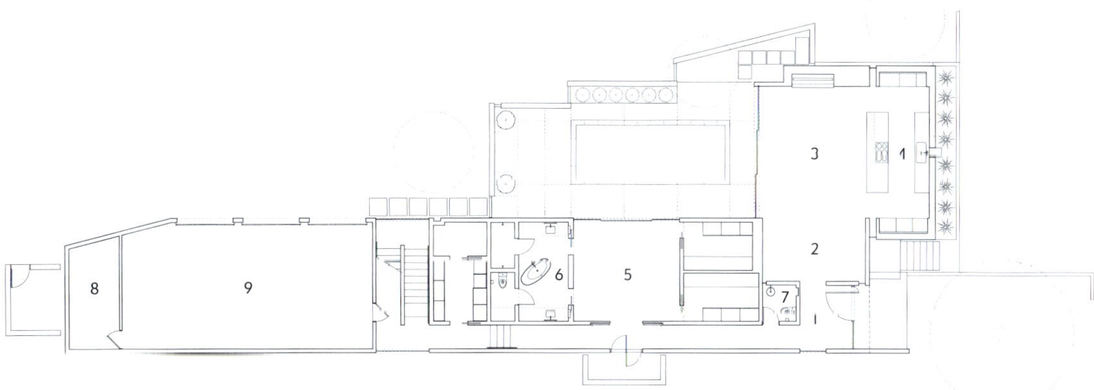


1 Entry
2 Dining room
3 Living room
4 Kitchen
5 Master bedroom
6 Master bathroom
7 Powder room
8 Storage
9 Garage

First-floor plan

0 20 ft

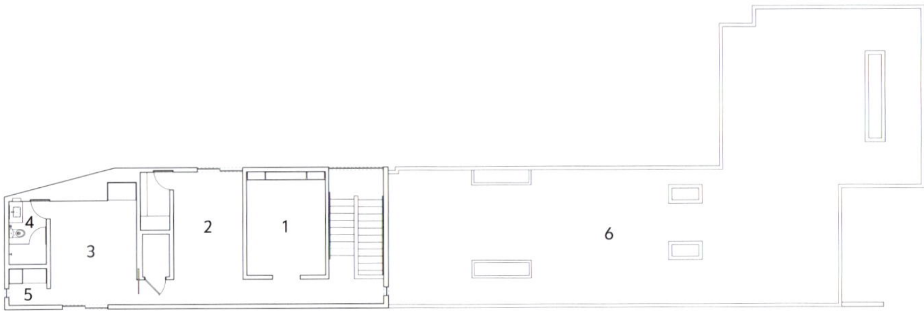

Second-floor plan

1 Media room
2 Study
3 Bedroom
4 Bathroom
5 Storage
6 Roof

0 20 ft

While the site features a natural slope, the design ensures that the main living spaces and master suite remain on a single level without steps, achieving seamless accessibility. Grade transitions are skillfully managed by cantilevered entry steps and steps connecting the house to the garage. The second floor accommodates a guest bedroom, office, and media room, accessed via a staircase offering scenic views of the garden and surrounding neighborhood.

The Avondale Residence exudes confidence and sophistication. With landscaping that celebrates the preserved oak tree and integrates guest parking on a natural grass surface, the home introduces itself gently to the neighborhood. Within, the design balances openness and intimacy, offering fluid transitions between spaces and an unparalleled connection to its private outdoor retreat.

## Bassi Ranch Residence

San Luis Obispo, California
2018

The Bassi Ranch Residence marks the third project designed and the second completed for this client. Nestled within the secluded Bassi Ranch development, the site offers breathtaking views of a lush valley and a wildlife-rich canyon. Dense plantings along the street create natural privacy, shielding the house from passing traffic.

Visitors are introduced to the home through an opening in the foliage, allowing the house to gradually reveal itself. Designated parking areas lead to an approach lined with vibrant 'Sango-kaku' Japanese maples, creating a serene approach to the front door.

Upon entering the vestibule, guests are welcomed into a central volume clad in Japanese sen wood. This space is designed to display art and a television while housing a discreet powder room, its presence hidden by a flush door and minimal hardware that seamlessly integrates with the sen wood.

Beyond this volume lies the main living area, elegantly connected to a canyon-facing porch. A continuous ceiling unites the interior and exterior spaces, while a full-height glass wall blurs the boundary between the two, creating the feeling of a single, unified space. A skylight spanning the length of the first floor provides natural light during the day, and integrated lighting subtly illuminates at night.

At one end of the house, the kitchen opens to a private courtyard that facilitates gardening, outdoor cooking, and dining. At the opposite end, the master suite and two home offices connect directly to the living space and porch, ensuring convenience and accessibility. While the main house includes only one bedroom, a guest apartment with a balcony is located above the garage, its structure piercing the freestanding front wall of the house.

Natural light floods every space through tall windows and skylights, offering views of either the private landscaped areas or the picturesque countryside.

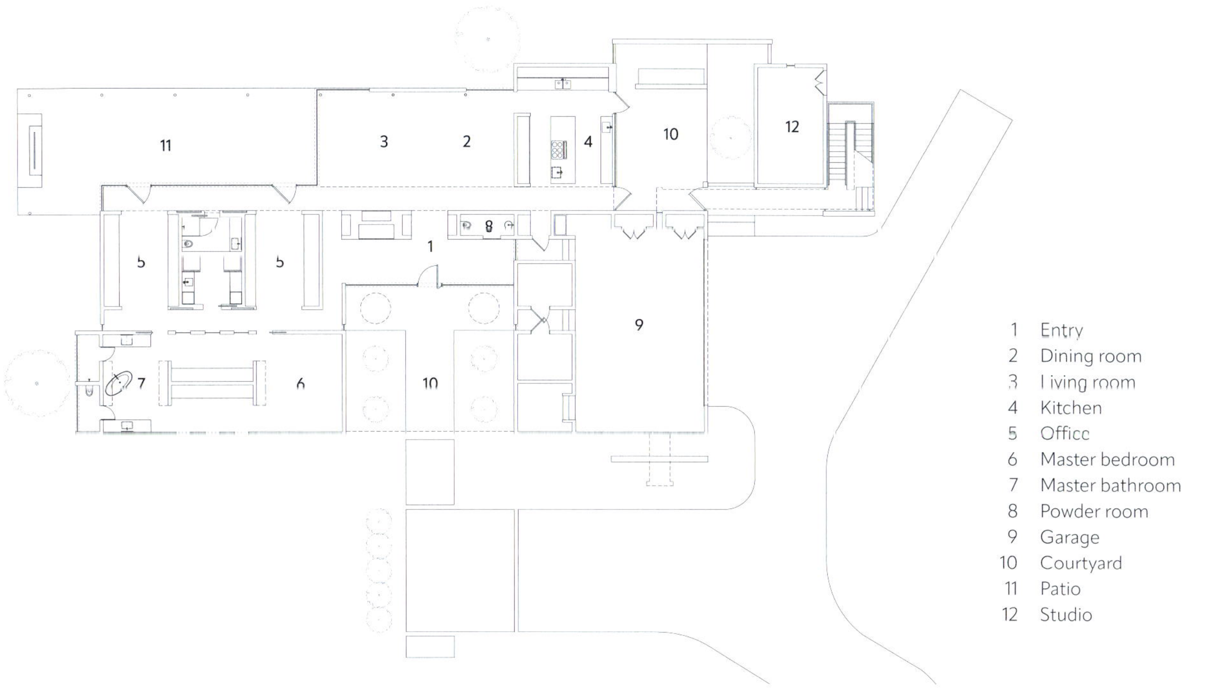


1 Entry
2 Dining room
3 Living room
4 Kitchen
5 Office
6 Master bedroom
7 Master bathroom
8 Powder room
9 Garage
10 Courtyard
11 Patio
12 Studio

First-floor plan

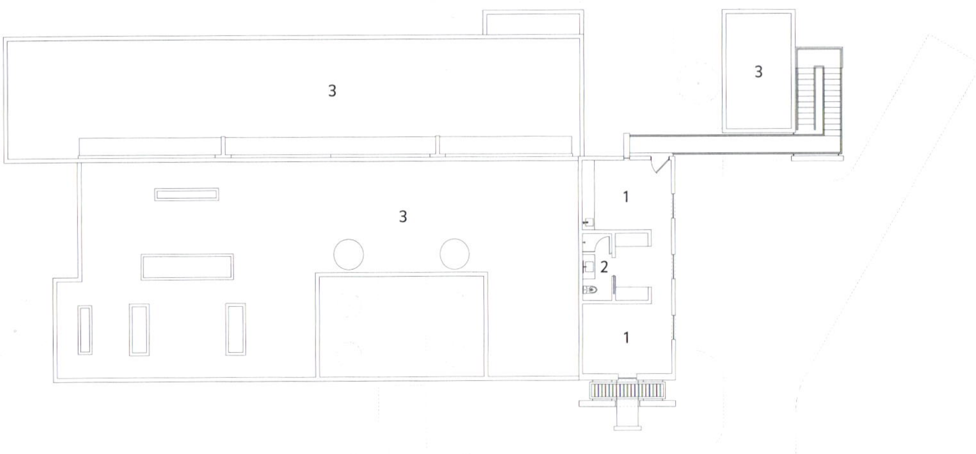


1 Bedroom
2 Bathroom
3 Roof

Second-floor plan

The material palette further enhances the seamless indoor–outdoor connection. The interior features diamond-polished concrete floors, while the porch employs concrete pavers set on a pedestal system. This design eliminates visible slopes and drains, maintaining consistent floor elevations, and extending the sense of cohesion between the interior and exterior environments.

The Bassi Ranch Residence capitalizes on its tranquil surroundings, offering an open and inviting retreat that harmonizes with its natural setting while providing a secure and elegant sanctuary for its owners.

# Brookview Residence

Dallas, Texas
2019

The Brookview Residence marks the second home designed for this couple, following the Berkshire Residence, also featured in this collection. This project expands upon the owners' program, introducing additional features such as a swimming pool, a portal with outdoor cooking facilities, and a games room. These requirements culminated in a 10,000-square-foot home, primarily on one level, that sits harmoniously on its heavily wooded, 2-acre site in the Sunnybrook Estates of Dallas.

The design reflects a continued affinity for courtyard-style homes, a preference shaped by the owners' satisfaction with their previous residence. This courtyard-centric layout is particularly well suited to the owners' lifestyle, which includes frequent entertaining of groups of varying sizes and showcasing their company's collection of outdoor furniture and fabrics.

Access to the residence is via a branching gravel driveway that leads guests to the porte cochere, while the owners are directed to the garage at the rear. Upon entering the vestibule, one can choose to proceed to the bedroom wing or ascend a few steps to reach the main living spaces. High windows allow natural light to fill the interior space, while maintaining privacy.

The living room serves as a gateway to the central courtyard, which features a pool and a flanking portal. Adjacent is the dining room, positioned along the pool's centerline, complete with its own intimate courtyard. Equipped with motorized wood screens, the dining room can be transformed into an enclosed or open space, lending itself to moments of theatricality when desired.

A strong visual axis is established along the pool's centerline, anchoring the surrounding functions. This axis extends through the house, culminating at the dining room garden at one end and a serene view of mature trees at the other. The portal, a favored gathering spot, includes an outdoor kitchen, bar, and television, all of which can be discreetly concealed when not in use.

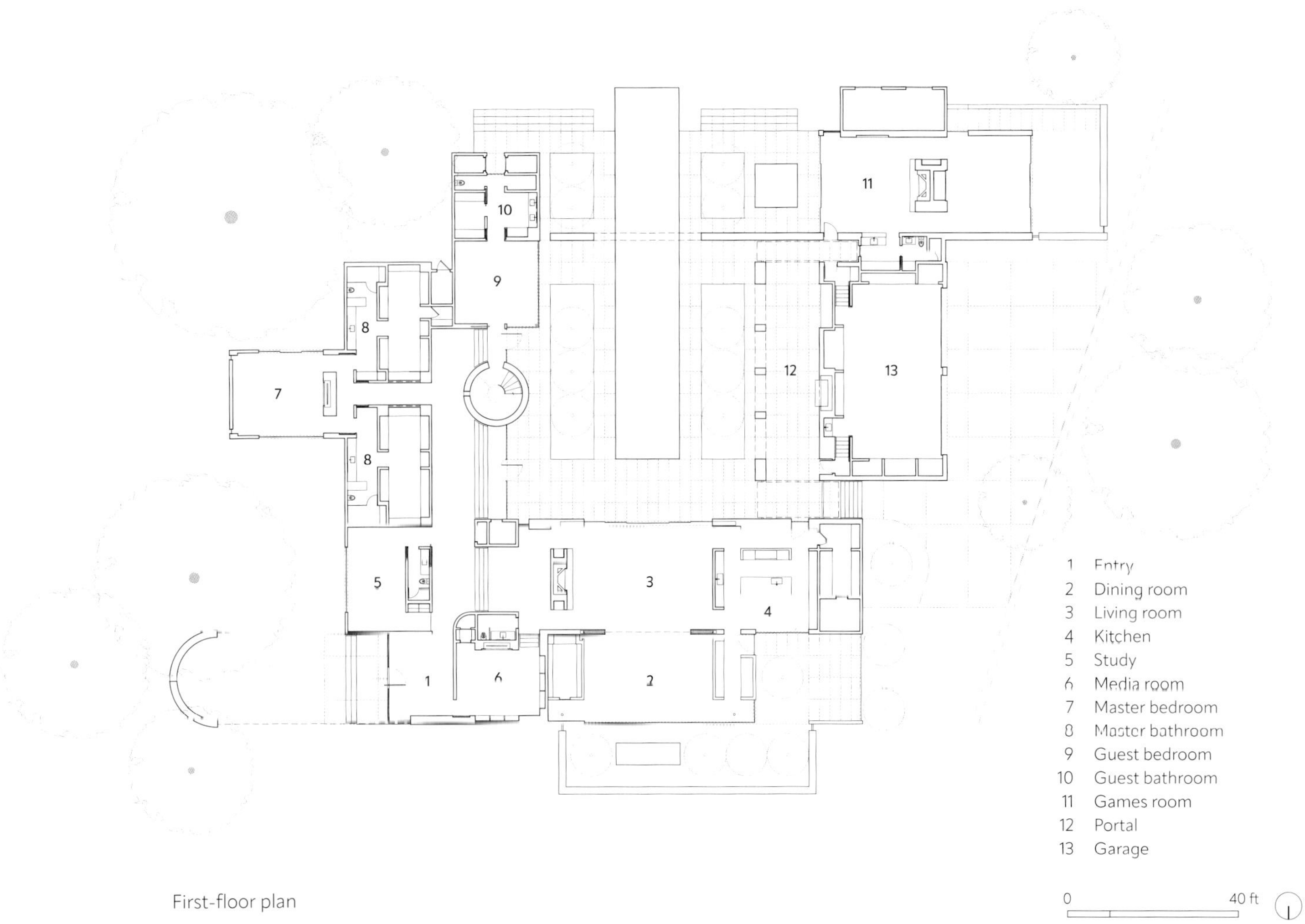


First-floor plan

The material palette enriches the residence's aesthetic, combining rough-cut limestone and gray-green stucco on the exterior walls with smooth, black granite slabs for flooring and courtyard surfaces. Blackened steel frames for windows and doors provide a striking contrast, while wood in various finishes adds warmth to floors, paneled walls, and exposed ceiling beams.

Notable features include courtyard paving that seamlessly aligns with interior flooring, installed on a pedestal system to eliminate cross-slopes and visible drains. The pool's water level aligns closely with the courtyard paving, enhancing the fluidity between indoor and outdoor spaces. Additionally, the staircase stringer, crafted from a single sheet of three-quarter-inch blackened steel plate, exemplifies a refined balance between strength and elegance.

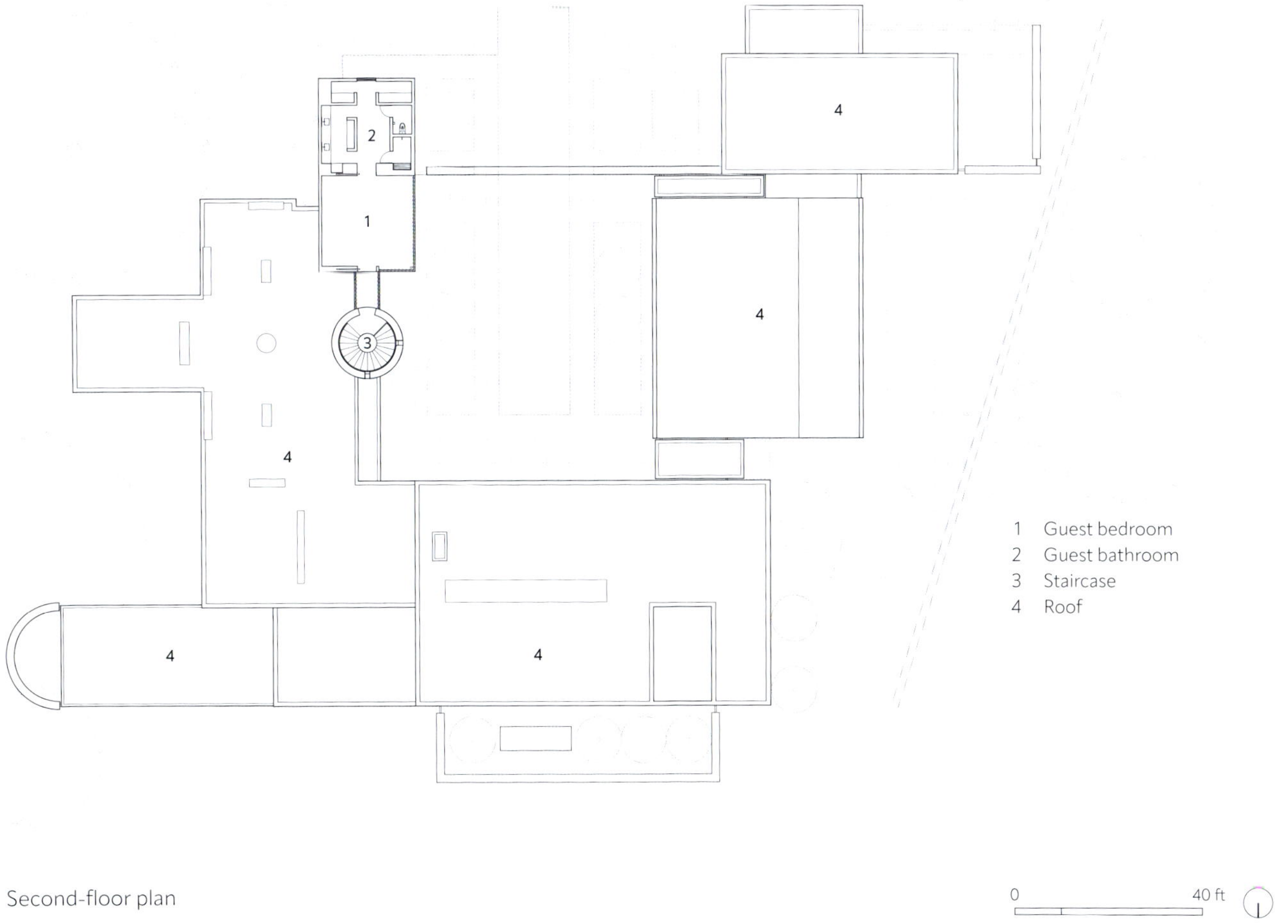


Second-floor plan

The Brookview Residence embodies the essence of a sophisticated country estate, modernized through its thoughtful arrangement, material richness, and the dynamic interplay of natural light that animates its spaces.

## Via Pampa Residence

Santa Fe, New Mexico
2024

The Via Pampa Residence is our second development in Santa Fe, following a residential condominium project in the Historic Design Review District downtown. Like its predecessor, this home was constructed within a neighborhood governed by rigorous design guidelines.

Situated in the Park Estates neighborhood of Las Campanas, this project pays homage to the Spanish Pueblo Revival style—widely recognized as the Santa Fe style. The community of Las Campanas is deeply committed to preserving this architectural legacy, and the homeowners actively uphold its principles. However, the Via Pampa Residence offers a modern interpretation of this cherished style. While often regarded as traditional and historic, the Santa Fe style inherently aligns with the tenets of modernism: rational programmatic solutions, integration of contemporary building technologies, efficient design and construction, a deliberate relationship with nature, and the absence of applied ornament.

At Via Pampa, traditional elements are thoughtfully reimagined. The Santa Fe style's distinctive features—such as canales (roof drains), vigas and latillas (roof framing members), and portals (porches)—are expressed as structural and visual ornament. For example, steel replaces wood in the canales, and trusses are highlighted through skylights, creating dynamic shadow play on the walls. Meanwhile, structural steel lintels at the portals, finished to match the window and door frames, form a cohesive ribbon that unites the home's architectural forms.

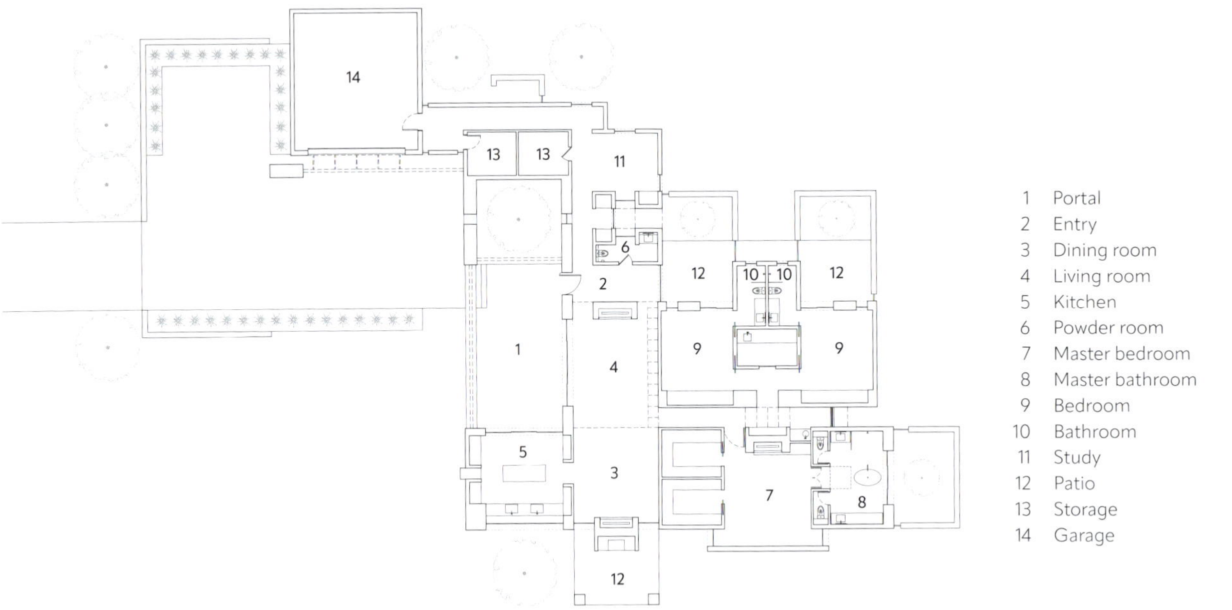


1 Portal
2 Entry
3 Dining room
4 Living room
5 Kitchen
6 Powder room
7 Master bedroom
8 Master bathroom
9 Bedroom
10 Bathroom
11 Study
12 Patio
13 Storage
14 Garage

Floor plan

Maximizing the stunning mountain views was a priority for this project. Portals and expansive glass walls are thoughtfully designed to frame vistas of the Sangre de Cristo Mountains, ensuring the surrounding landscape becomes an integral part of the home's experience.

The journey into the residence begins under the main portal, where guests are greeted by an Aspen courtyard and outdoor living space. Upon entry, curated views of outdoor sculptures and specimen maple trees—with vibrant orange foliage in the fall—unfold, enhancing the home's connection to nature.

Inside, the living and dining area features fireplaces at both ends and dramatic views of the Sangre de Cristo Mountains. The centrally located kitchen seamlessly connects the dining room to the main portal, making it ideal for entertaining. An intimate north-facing portal provides additional outdoor cooking and dining options, with unparalleled sunset views of the Jemez Mountains.

The master suite opens onto a private courtyard, which can also be accessed from the bathroom, thanks to sliding glass panels that disappear into the walls. Each guest suite enjoys its own courtyard, offering views of the Jemez Mountains and a nearby park—one of the beautifully maintained amenities of Las Campanas.

## Afterword

by Lionel Morrison

Architecture can be understood as the art of problem-solving with an aesthetic agenda. The challenges to be addressed arise from the context—this encompasses the site, the program, and any other factors influencing the design of the structure.

As a committed modernist, I adhere to the core principles of modernism: a rational response to the building program where form follows function, the use of contemporary and available building materials and technologies, an economy of means in both design and construction, and the avoidance of applied ornamentation. By remaining steadfast to these principles and thoughtfully addressing the context of each project, I have produced a consistent and distinguished body of work.

The houses presented in this collection share similar or even identical building programs, yet each exhibits a strikingly unique appearance. This uniqueness stems entirely from my response to the specific context of each house.

While distinct contexts yield distinct solutions, those with a discerning eye can unmistakably recognize my work. The recognition arises from the consistent methodology employed to address design challenges—a philosophy that is physically manifested in every final product.

Morrison's distinctive interpretation of modernist principles features throughout his many works, including Stonebridge Residence, as displayed opposite and on page 143.

# Architect Profile

Lionel Morrison, FAIA

Lionel Morrison's residential and commercial work has been consistently recognized by his peers, with over thirty design awards. He has served on design juries throughout the Southwest and lectured at various universities and associations.

Morrison gained a Bachelor of Arts from the University of Texas at Austin and a Master of Architecture from the University of Texas at Arlington. In 1992, his first year of eligibility, Morrison was elevated to the American Institute of Architects' College of Fellows. Four years later he was named a Distinguished Alumnus by the School of Architecture at the University of Texas at Arlington. The following year he was named the Outstanding Architect by the American Society of Interior Designers.

Morrison started his firm in 1982 and has produced exceptional work in Texas, New Mexico, Georgia, Florida, and California. His current focus is on designing and developing homes for purchase in Santa Fe, New Mexico—where he now lives—while continuing to accept private architectural commissions there and elsewhere.

# Awards and Recognition

### Texas Society of Architects Design Awards

Sutherland Residence

Travis Street Houses

Kovach Residence

Travis Street Condominiums

Armstrong Avenue Townhouses

Roberdeau Residence

### American Institute of Architects Design Awards

Abbott Residence

Northaven Residence

One Arts Plaza

Berkshire Residence

Versailles Residence

International Business Park

Travis Street Houses

Preston Hollow Residence

Glendora II Residence

Princeton Residence

Lebowitz Townhouses

Fidelity Bank

Distinguished Architect Exhibit

Travis Street Condominiums

Springbrook Avenue Townhouses

Roberdeau Residence

2811 McKinney

Armstrong Avenue Townhouses

### *D Magazine* Recognition of Excellence

2019, 25 Year Most Beautiful Home in Dallas, Beechwood Residence

2008, 10 Most Beautiful Homes in Dallas, Versailles Residence

2004, Home of the Year Merit Award, Sutherland Residence

2003, Home of the Year, Versailles Residence

2002, Urban Home of the Year, Travis Street Townhouses

### *PaperCity* Design Awards

2018, Commercial Landscape Design, Eagle Family Plaza at the Dallas Museum of Art

2016, Residential Architectural Design Under 3500 Square Feet, Arthouse Apartment 3A

### Topping Out Awards

2017, Top Ten Award, Eagle Family Plaza at the Dallas Museum of Art

### Urban Land Institute North Texas Impact Awards

2017, Public Places Award, Eagle Family Plaza at the Dallas Museum of Art

# Acknowledgments

We have had the great fortune of collaborating with wonderful clients, those who trust and support us while challenging us to do our best. We would like to recognize those whose projects appear in this book: Steve and Karen Levine; Craig Kovach; Terry and Janet Kafka; David and Ann Sutherland; Dennis and Rosemary Heard; Diane and Chuck Cheatham; Robert Moore and Terry Thompson; Robert Hallam; Lucilo Peña and Lee Cobb; Steve Silesky and Jacqui Ghosin; Steve and Ellen Miller.

We would also like to recognize other important clients whose projects are not shown in this book but whose contributions to our body of work are undeniable: Roblee McCarthy; Michael and Sandra Roberdeau; Josy and Marty Collins; Alan Kagan; Logan Waller; Brant McFarlain and Justin Moon.

None of the results shown herein would have been possible without the efforts of our talented staff. Thank you to those who contributed significantly to these works: Rocky Owens; Wes Tunnell; Joanna Hampton; Dan Eckelkamp; Deanne Teeter; Jennifer Harralson; Brant McFarlain.

## Photography

Our considerable appreciation extends to our long-time collaborator Charles Davis Smith, whose expert photography has captured the majority of our projects. Many of these photographs are featured throughout this book. Thanks also go to Peter Aaron, who contributed the photography of the Beechwood Residence (pp. 10–15) and the Princeton Residence (pp. 16–21), Pete Ayer who photographed the Bassi Ranch Residence (pp. 106–113), and Douglass Friedman for his photography of Stonebridge Residence (pp. 139 and 143).

Published in Australia in 2026 by
The Images Publishing Group Pty Ltd
ABN 89 059 734 431

Offices

| *Melbourne* | *New York* | *Shanghai* |
|---|---|---|
| Waterman Business Centre | 6 West 18th Street 4B | 6F, Building C, 838 Guangji Road |
| Suite 64, Level 2 UL40 | New York City, NY 10011 | Hongkou District, Shanghai 200434 |
| 1341 Dandenong Road | United States | China |
| Chadstone, Victoria 3148 | Tel: +1 212 645 1111 | Tel: +86 021 31260822 |
| Australia | | |
| Tel: +61 3 8564 8122 | | |

books@imagespublishing.com
www.imagespublishing.com


The Images Publishing Group Reference Number: IM1754

All photography is attributed on page 142, unless otherwise noted. Front cover: Charles Davis Smith (Brookview Residence); back cover: Charles Davis Smith (Avondale Residence); page 4: Charles Davis Smith (Via Pampa Residence); page 140: Charles Davis Smith (Lionel Morrison portrait).



A catalogue record for this book is available from the National Library of Australia

Title: Modernism in Context: Homes by Lionel Morrison
Author: Lionel Morrison
ISBN: 9781923094062

This title was commissioned in IMAGES' Melbourne office and produced as follows: *Design and project management* Ryan Marshall; *Editorial* Helen Koehne, Jeanette Wall; *Proofreading* Rebecca Gross; *Production* Simon Walsh, Heather Johnson; *Prepress* A & S Graphics (Singapore)

EU GPSR Authorised Representative: Easy Access System Europe Oü
Company Registration ID: 16879218 | Address: Mustamäe tee 50, 10621 Tallinn, Estonia
Email: gpsr@easproject.com | Tel: +358 40 500 3575

MIX
Paper | Supporting responsible forestry
FSC® C008047

Printed on 157gsm Chinese Hua Xia Sun (FSC) matt art paper by C&C Offset Printing Co., Ltd.